# Poetry Diversified

*An Anthology of Human Experience*

## 2012 Winners
### of the Poetry Matters Literary Prize

*Introduction by Ali Fry*
*Compiled by Lucinda J. Clark*

Poetry Diversified: An Anthology of Human Experience

Copyright @ 2013 P.R.A. Publishing

ISBN: 0984014233
ISBN 13: 9780984014231 print
LCCN: 2013906942
P R A Publishing, Martinez, G.A.

Cover design by NewFire Media
www.newfiremedia.com
Copyright used with permission of the artist
Printed and bound in the U.S.A

Published by
P.R.A. Publishing
P.O. Box 211701,
Martinez, Georgia 30917
www.prapublishing.com

*"We have become not a melting pot but a beautiful mosaic. Different people, different beliefs, different yearnings, different hopes, different dreams."*

-Jimmy Carter-

# Acknowledgements

It is with each passing year that I become more and more gracious while completing this section of the Poetry Matters anthology. There are so many people to thank for making this book and our growing contest possible year after year.

I would like to first thank our sponsors. Center for Primary Care has provided cash prizes since the contest's inception, and the Aiken Standard has been a steadfast sponsor for at least three consecutive years. I would also like to say thank you to P.R.A. Publishing for providing the muscle that keeps things on track.

We simply could not make Poetry Matters possible without our dedicated judges. This year, Jessica Clark and Lisa Rosier judged the middle school category, and we utilized the skills of Xavier Clark, Lucinda Clark and Sharon Schroeder for the high school category. For the adult category, Gina Behr, Takisha Perry and Donna Weir-Soley were kind enough to be judges, and NC Weil, Collin Kelley and Ira Harrison, PhD, worked hard on the senior category.

For the last two years, we have had talented interns from the Communications Department of Georgia Regents University aiding us in creating our anthologies. These young people have taken the concept of showcasing emerging poetic voices to a new level. This year, I have had the pleasure of working with Ali Fry; you will see her creative talents in the introduction and cover design. She also secured the services of NewFire Media; they designed the cover of Poetry Diversified and our new website which has taken us to new heights.

Last but not least I must thank Professors Terri Sasser and Anthony Kellman for providing us with great interns, and Robert Clark DO for maintaining our website which showcases the contest winners reading their works of art.

Thanks to you all. As always, we couldn't do what we do if you didn't do what you do!

# Table of Contents

# Introduction

As badly as I want to fill this introduction with glittering adjectives and entertaining wit, I must refrain. This anthology is not about the language in the introduction. It's about the readers and the poets themselves. It's about humanity as a whole and the beauty of experiences poetically and humbly expressed.

At the beginning of this process, I was presented with a stack of poems and asked to sort them. I had no idea where to begin, and quickly made the foolish assumption that a two-worded demand would require very little effort on my part; but as I began to read, every word spoke to me and touched me in a million different ways. It took no time at all for the theme of this anthology to dawn on me: diversity. These writers represent variations in age, race, gender, religion and every type of social category, and, in turn, their diverse experiences represent that.

Suddenly, I knew I had to do the writing justice and order the poems in a poetic way. I allowed the phrases, metaphors and experiences to guide my hands as I organized the poems into chapters according to the experiences they represented.

At first, I found my plan to be ingenious and felt as if I was giving the poems worthy beds in which to lie. Unfortunately, and ironically, I ended up realizing that twenty-three different experiences do not house enough similarities to be grouped into a mere four or five separate categories. I didn't understand that I needed to think a bit less like a writer and more like an intern, and I definitely shouldn't have attempted to make art out of art instead of simply giving the art a frame.

After surviving that part of my experience, there were still millions of technical decisions to be made: the font on the front of this anthology, the font on the back, the font in between, the sizes of all this font, the copyright page, the positioning of the poets' names, the type of paper used, etc.; and this is but a fraction of what has to be thought. With all these technical questions whirling around in my head, it was hard to see through it to the finished product; but here it is, art framed with details formed by an intern.

Poetry Diversified is filled with language bearing the souls of twenty-three poets with twenty-three different stories to tell. My greatest wish for you while perusing this anthology is that you are able to read these diverse human experiences and soak in the sorrow, guilt, discovery, hope, and joy that I consumed while diving into one of the greatest opportunities: constructing a masterpiece that was already a masterpiece. Enjoy.

-Ali Fry-

# MIDDLE SCHOOL WINNERS

# LIFE ON A PAPER

I can't wait 'til the day when
I can say that I am happy!
Not happy as in some random guy
just kissed me in the rain,
And we replayed the movie over and over again,
But happy as in I looked in the mirror, and
all I could do was smile.
All I could do was smell the sweet,
unfamiliar scent of confidence.

Happy as I was comfortable with my body,
I was comfortable with the shape and size of my breasts, the
swerve of my hips,
the cellulite on my ass,
the stretch marks climbing to my waist,
the cuts on my wrist.

I was comfortable with my unstraightened hair
or even my Monday morning dry lips.
And I was blessed.
Blessed as in I am thankful
for everything God gave me,

thanking him for another day,
getting on my knees, bowing my head and
asking him to keep predators away.

Looking at my mom and embracing her smile,
looking at my stepdad for awhile
and thinking to myself,
that's what you call a good guy.
I wanna wake up
with a joyous thrill crawling through my feet.
Tickling the dead ends of my hair,
hitting the rooftops of my lungs
with an effect of a horror tune.
Falling so fast down my arms, that I'm numb,
and the only thing I can touch
is the happiness in the air.

Walking around the snowflakes and sunlight,
and the whole botanical garden
just below my underwear.

I wanna walk outside with no makeup,
extensions, and no shirt,
no pants, a headscarf and no bra,
telling the world that I'm real
and suggest the idea to them, too.

I'll even put on a new pair of shoes.
Shoes that walk miles where I may be alone.
Miles that might not have the greatest clothes
or best food to swallow.
A mile where I don't know what's tomorrow.
A mile where the leaves, snake and grass all sing a song so sweet
to the earth —

Wind and fire begin to weep.
A mile that isn't so green but isn't so grey.
A mile where I get on my knees, lift my voice and say,
"I am happy and I am alive.
I do have voice, so listen.
I do have eyes, so show me where the free birds sing.
I do have ears, so let me hear that glory street is near.
I do have a heart that's less filled with fear."
I just can't wait 'til I'm happy,
'Til I can embrace true beauty,
And I can accept who I am.

But until then I'll find myself
drawing self-portraits with smiles
and phony quotes of confidence
written in Sharpie on school notebooks,

reciting Maya Angelo's poem
"Still I Rise" backwards in my mind,
and guess what? Instead of cutting my wrist
with crooked lines,
I'll carve words such as
beautiful, perspicuous and perfect
to make it all worth it.

I'll trace happiness into
the great Sahara desert with my bare feet.
I may even take a picture and upload it to Twitter.
I'll walk down every road,
on every street and every block,

searching and looking for Happiness Avenue.
And if I still can't find that happy place
that I plead to call home,
I'll just sit on my bed, open my journal
and grab a pen
And continue creating my own.

Lauren Welch
Miami, FL
I$^{st}$ Place

# TEARDROPS

I sat on the cold pavement.
Muddy tears ran down my cheek.
The rain trickled down faster;
So did my tears and in every teardrop,
There was a memory.

In one drop;
I saw the chicken seasoned lightly,
Resting on our plates; I saw the smiles
In the homemade french-fries,
crispy and salty on the edges.
The meal splashed into the puddle.

Next drop; our house was filled with portraits of us;
Together, happy as a family.
Splash!
The memory slowly dispersed in the water.

In another drop, I saw the front view of our house;
A white door with a cheerful "Welcome" sign.

Inside we were playing Monopoly,
One of my favorites.
Then the walls started to crumble,
and the ceiling collapsed; into the puddle.

It felt like yesterday when I thought
Those memories would last forever.

"We're gonna make it through this," Mom whispered.
There was no warmth in her eyes; they were hollow.
Filled with the desire of lasagna layered with Comforting
parmesan cheese.
She said the economy was bad;
I didn't think we'd be affected.

I closed my eyes
And felt the tattered rags hugging my body.
My stomach was screaming.
I would do anything for food.
Anything for a home.
Anything to feel whole again.

I sit on the cold pavement;
Feeling my dreams trampled and forgotten.
Muddy tears run down my cheek.
And hope evaporates.

Emma Cuba
Biscayne Park, FL
2nd Place

# THE LOUD SOUND OF THE DOOR SLAMMING

Lying in my room, tiny music buds buzzing in my ear,
I heard the screams of vicious beasts.
It started with a conversation, as usual,
Quickly turning into a fight.
Momma started crying, daddy started screaming.

Tears came to my eyes
As my fingers stroked the dial on my iPod,
But no matter how high the volume,
I couldn't escape it.
I couldn't block the sound out.
Then I heard it,
The loud sound of the door slamming.

Life went straight downward from there.
My mom hardly ever talks, and
The joy that used to fill the house is gone.
It was as if an old friend
Ran away with my dad that night.

After that, it was as if a dark cloud surrounded me.
Life seems meaningless and empty
Like the vacant house across the street.

.

Lying in my room, tiny music buds buzzing in my ear
All I hear, now, is the loud sound of the door slamming.

Katherine Nichols
Miami Shores, FL
3rd Place

# IF I HAD A PUSH BROOM

If I had a push broom
I'd push away all my pain
Soon to be returned as words of kindness.

If I had a vacuum broom
I'd suck up all my troubles
And distribute them to each ray of sun
Soon to be returned as droplets of happiness.

If I had a tall broom
I'd climb up to a world unknown
Not knowing what will be returned.

If I had a broom made of moonlight
I'd throw it to the sky
Soon to be returned as a nightlight.

If I had a broom made of glass
I'd shatter each bristle
Soon to be returned as a lesson learned.

If I had a broom made of paint
I'd paint the floor
Soon to be returned as artwork.

If I had a broom made of grass
I'd plant each one
Soon to be returned as a garden.

If I had a broom made of feathers
I'd pluck each one
Soon to be returned as a new life.

As I awaken
a closet of  brooms  stands before me.
This is where the revolution of brooms began.

Hadassah Amani
Miami, FL
4th Place

# HIGH SCHOOL WINNERS

# SOLDIER'S WAR

This is hell.
There are no applicable adjectives.
They've been through training.
That was tough.
This is death's doorstep.

The mud is no problem.
They've been wading knee-deep for days.
The crowded trenches are familiar.
They've been living on top of each other for days.
The pain is nonexistent.
They've gritted their teeth through it for days.
They don't notice it anymore.

The hell is the cloud of hopelessness that
No one can escape.

They can trudge through covered in filth and grime,
But they cannot raise their spirits.
They can huddle on top of each other
As blasts fall all around,
But they cannot even dream of a future.
They can cry through the night
To forget about the pain,
But they cannot find motivation.

War
The black hole of hope,
Will this ever end
Of everything joyous,
Will they see their loved ones
Of reason and understanding.
Why are they risking their lives
To kill another man, another human

A young boy confesses,
I'm scared to die.
A companion replies,
What do you want me to do.
A veteran interrupts,
There is no escape.

War
This inescapable hell.
This vacuum that makes you
Forget  the good in the world.
This eraser of warm memories of mothers
And sisters and girlfriends.
This monster that devours and engulfs the soul.

When they return,
If they return,
They are forever changed.
They've been through hell.

Olivia Zhao
Overland Park, KS
I$^{st}$ Place

# BLACKBIRDS

## I. Her

Blackbirds fluttered through her hair,
Their tail feathers
Catching in her curls
And dyeing the strands black.
Ink dripped from her eyes
And boiled the snow
Where she stood,
Utterly alone.

## II. Him

He watched her curiously
As the snow fell lightly
Upon the written ink of his pen.
He imagined blackbirds
Streaming from the silent winter sky
And landing upon her,
Softly and delicately as their tail feathers
Wiped away her tears.

## III. Them

Their eyes met.
And the snow caught between them,
A simple breath,

Held.
A sudden sentiment,
Slipping from their lips like
Glossy ink.
And the soft touch of skin,
Like the stroke of a tail feather,
The offering of a blackbird,
As they slid into a kiss.

Brittany Crow
Woodbridge, VA
2nd Place

# "PLEASE, MOM, DON'T GO."

A toddler in the playroom
Content with his toys
His mother has to go to the store
She kisses his forehead and goes to the door
But he grabs her hand and shakes it
And says in his child-like voice
"Pwease, Mommy, don't go."

A boy on his first day
Third grade can be daunting
She walks him to his class and says goodbye
But he stops her and looks her in the eyes
His face is red and his knees are shaking as he says
"Please, Mom, don't go."

A teenager now, she drops him off at a friend's house
She mentions the game and
would like to come see him play

But his friends will be there
And she might embarrass him
And after a long argument
he gets out of the car and yells
"PLEASE MOM! DON'T GO!"

In a hospital room
She lies in the bed
He's a man now, with a wife and kids

She's old and frail and he holds her hand
The monitor beeps and beeps,
then the long sustained sound

He squeezes her hand and begins to cry
He whispers to himself
"Please, mom ... don't go."

Ryan Looft
New Paltz, NY
3rd Place

# AIM

My father wants me to join the military.
He wants me to go to West Point
and become a sniper.
So every year at Christmas time, he
takes the bow and arrow
outside to the front yard,
attaches fishing line on the end
and tells me to aim.
I try to tell him that
I don't want to be a soldier.
I want to be a poet
or an artist
or a mermaid.
He ties the Christmas lights
to the end of the fishing line
and tells me to aim.
He swears it's not for training.
He swears it's just the easiest way
to get the lights
all the way up the tree.
Every year he brings out
the thick, black hunting bow
and the arrow with quarters
taped to the end.
He puts it in my hands
and tells me to aim.
I lift the bow high,

pull the thin arrow back,
so the foam feathers on the end
brush my cheekbones,

Aim.
Release.
Perfection, nearly every time.
It wraps around the branches,
and we pull the sparkling lights to the top,
walking them around and around,
so they twist like candy canes.

My father reminds me the West Point application
will be due soon.
He tells me I need to aim high, shoot to kill.
I toss the bow to the ground
and grab hold of his hands.
I tell him his aim is off.
I spin him around to face my future,
bright and twinkling.
As it winds up the tree and into the sky.

Grace Henderson
Allendale, NJ
4th Place

# HIGH SCHOOL-CSRA WINNERS

# TO A FALLEN COMRADE

i want to be the soil beneath your twisted bones
that rises to cradle you like a tired mother,
drinking in the life force drained from your body,
savoring this and all that you have lost

— it would taste like a single drop of salt water
on a desert journey.

you will soon look upon the faces of the saints
as i will know the faces of one thousand more
of our enemies.  in the purest whites of their eyes
i seek a holy power;
i clutch your tags like a rosary.

i will never again watch the sun set behind your shoulder,
through your hair
as you speak to me of your frail sister in Connecticut,
but i will hear your clumsy footsteps in the crush of the Atlantic
and fancy that you are strolling beside.

and even though

i know that the sun still sets,
and that without a parting glance i must march on,
tonight i will lie awake
pulsing,
and breathing, and restlessly wondering

if you died knowing —
if you ever knew —

i love the stars that made you, and
i love the earth that will take you back.

Lyndsey Wilcox
Augusta, GA
I[st] Place

# ALL I SEEK

Under the spotlight scrutinized by hundreds
Thousands
Maybe even a million and two,
The expectation level to perform is higher than ever.
"Don't let them down," I tell myself.
"Don't mess up," I command my calloused, aching fingers.
"Please accept me for who I am," a tiny voice in my head
whispers so quietly
Even a ghost would struggle to make out the words.
But finally, it's over.
All smiles in the audience, save one, reveal my great triumph as a
young Juilliard star.
An almost flawless performance in my eyes,
But unfortunately, I don't share the same opinion as the small
pointed Japanese woman at my house.
"Your G sharp too sharp! Shorter staccatos in Vivace section of
Sarasate!
Need more practice before recital tomorrow."
But how can I practice any more than I already am?
Three hours a day is ample practice time for a fifteen-year-old,
right?
I argue back, but I always get the same response back:
"You Pre-Juilliard Artist because you young and you good.
Aim for better."
It's sickly religious how she preaches that one line to me
Day in and day out—
But how can I possibly be better than my best?

How can I make her proud of me?
Perfection.
Perfection.
Perfection.
Once again, I tuck the Stradivarius beneath my chin where my
violin bruise is a sickly blackened purple
I curl my calloused fingers around the neck of the violin ready to
practice until…
Until…
Who cares anymore?
Perfection is all I seek, yet I'll never reach it.
I'd love to have a break from the hundreds of hours of practicing
and rehearsing,
But I'd also love to have my mother's approval that I'm good
enough.

Kendall Driscoll
Aiken, SC
2ⁿᵈ Place

# COLLISION

We are all barreling down a hill
In a soapbox car race
Where the finish line is death.
Faced with inevitability, we speed.
Our theft of first and second place
Seems sometimes unfair.
We make all the jumps and wrong turns
To get there first.

But sometimes we collide,
Wooden frames smashing into each other.
Side-swiping at breakneck speeds,
We bounce off each other like
Atoms causing an explosion,
Causing the erosion of the walls that confine us,
That line us in rows.
Forced through a maze
Careful with selection.
Because sometimes if we walk down the right paths,
We make a connection.

Together, we must let go of gravity
Because it's all that's been holding us down
In the cavity of heart's travesty,
Like we're still smoothing out the imprints

Other soapbox cars left on our frames.
Where they bent the wood and warped it
Where they dent your heart now haunted,
They crushed the brave, now daunted.

Death, it seems, tastes a lot like fame,
But gunpowder and ash taste about the same.
What heavenly clock decides our fates?

I write all the endings myself,
Well-schemed climaxes to decimate.
It's all planned out from the start
To break someone's heart
Or skull if we're bad enough drivers.
I am the mouse.
I am the mousetrap.
The alpha and omega.
The victim and the bullet.
The postcard and the insincere inscription.
Cutting string too soon,
Losing thoughts on purpose
Like a man willing to drown himself
After each reincarnation.
Perpetual self-immolation.

We spend our lives crashing into each other,
Every collision causing an impact,
Rehashing another accident.
And if I swerve into you in the future,

I beg I won't make too bad a dent
Because when it comes to people,
Much like with books,
It matters less about the appearance
And more about the content.

We live lives where death is permitted,
Even encouraged to some degree,
Because, you see, to not die would break
The sincere system that everyone lives by
Where Home becomes that place
You go when you can't go too far,
And memories become parables we tell ourselves
To remind us who we are.

You wonder if anybody slows down
To take it all in.
Instead of faking it too much,
Instead of shaking your head
And crossing your arms
Like snowmen who freeze through the night,
Like the zeitgeist of time travelers.
The clocks spin madly, and I'm left the only one
Who reads ever the sonnets of a setting sun.

I have seen in my days
Some pretty traumatic car wrecks
Where necks snapped and hearts broke.
The blind saw, the mutes spoke

And some of us stood up
And said, "Don't worry, we're fine."
Didn't realize we'd already crossed
The finish line.

Derek Berry
Aiken, SC
3rd Place

# ADULT WINNERS

# ROOM 232

There are pretty rooms in this hospital,
rooms with wallpaper borders and fabric valances
over windows framing a sweeping view of
the surrounding hills and heaven-bound steeples,
rooms with custom built closets and shelves
and mirrors to see yourself smile.

This room is not one of them. This room is
yellow. Tired yellow. Not the yellow of sunrise
or ducks or spring balloons but the same yellow as
the chair in the corner, the spotted linoleum on the floor,
the metal inserts dividing the ceiling tiles.

This room looks out over the graveled rooftop of
the elevator shaft, whirling turbines the only testament
to fresh air. This room feels like a room where
old people die, and he's in it, and I'm in it, and
there's no turning back.

There is a framed print on the wall of two white swans gliding
through a turquoise stream surrounded by spring
blooming plants
in pinks and yellows and
anchored by a solid stone bridge crossing from one
peaceful shore to the other and

I wonder if we're supposed to be the swans,
gliding gently from one world into the next, surrounded by peace
and pastel harmony without ever seeing the hunter in the bushes,
hiding, waiting,
hungry, and raw.

Sally Clark
Fredericksburg, TX
I<sup>st</sup> Place

# GIVE AND TAKE

He gave his youth to his country.
They gave him an education.

He gave a sprinter's leg.
They gave him a prosthetic.

He gave his gut to a grenade.
They gave him an ostomy bag,
the opening pitch, box seats,
and a standing ovation.

When he gave his sanity, too,
he got the runaround.

He took his life, and, in the end,
they gave his mother a flag.

J.C. Elkin
Annapolis, MD
2nd Place

# RELUCTANT INTERVENTION

take keys away from the man
picturing himself in his '60 Chevy
fins and chrome and shiny hood ornament
wife hides behind her cat's-eye shades
scarf on her head like Grace Kelly to his
Cary Grant. Windows half-mast as tendrils of
cigarette smoke escape. AM radio blares
kids argue over stance on the hump
trunk filled with beach paraphernalia
plus spare tire

He drove since age fourteen
gas guzzlers with distinction.
Satisfying door thunk
not today's tink

youngsters grew up, drive bland SUVs
convene in kitchen to yank his
American dream

Joanne Faries
Bedford, TX
3rd Place

# KOI

What if Albert was right?
What if what we call time
is not the river that carries
us towards the future, a natural
spring, the essence of our lives,
a fountain of experience
for us to bathe under and
bask, until we leave certain
of never coming back?

What if Albert was right, what if
time is but a pond, immovable,
peaceful, and eternal,
that contains the universe?
What if instead of swimming
against the current, believing
we can beat the odds, all
we beat is ourselves?

If Albert was right, if time is, in fact,
not a river, but a pond,
then we are not the challengers
of fate, the gladiators of destiny,
the invincible masters of life,
but multicolored
fish, swimming in our little
corner of the universe,

following the light, chasing
little morsels the world
throws on the surface,
convinced that those tiny
specs are all there is, and not realizing
there's a whole universe inside the pond.

Marilyn Marquez
Agawam, MA
4th Place

# ADULT-CSRA WINNERS

# OATHS & PSALMS

Evening, early solstice—the greater
of two lights reflects on adding day spin
to the sun; still ruminant and in the dark
about the weather. A single Carolina

rosebush awaits her yellow ribbons,
and that first dance beside a sipping
stream. I am not a warrior poet—
musicians are passive men—byline

silhouettes with twenty-dollar bills
and slices of frozen pizza. I will not offer
you vinegar on a sponge at the point
of a spear or track your rem sleep

from sleuth shadows—there are trimmed
candles in my pocket—I plant tulip
bulbs in snowmelt. Oaths are like psalms.
Flesh is never weak that wets a finger

in the wind, to divine a way to share
another's burden—death can only break
the vows we pledge to let it part.

Kevin Heaton
Aiken, SC
I<sup>st</sup> Place

# BLACK BOYS

"I don't like boys calling,"
she said with a solemn stare
as if the role of motherhood
glued us together in mandatory camaraderie.

Then, with squinty lifeless eyes, she whispered,
"Especially black boys."

Black boys.
Words she murmured so low
as if she feared an underground SWAT team were
assigned strictly to those who uttered them.

Black boys.
As if pronouncing it aloud would
instantly display her phone number
to each one who existed.

"That boy just keeps calling my girl," she said.

I started to respond,
"But I know him. He's an honor…"
Then stopped instead to gaze in wonder
at the cigarette dangling
from her flappy lips,
thumbs tucked toughly into floral embroidered pockets
as if extra attention was needed

for pants already so tight
that she appeared bound to them forever.
I wondered what heroic display of strength
would be necessary to remove them.
Maybe only that of a
strong black boy.

I itched to scream out,
"Black boys!"
"Black boys!"
"Black boys!"

Resounding,
so that each white neighbor would be forced to hear.
I pondered the outcome, imagining
that hundreds of brawny brown-skinned boys
would exit the woodwork of my lily white surroundings
and come running to arrest her,
their own SWAT team reacting only
to the words "Black Boys"
when whispered.

Darlena Moore
Evans, GA
2<sup>nd</sup> Place

# MY LEGACY

From the moment you were in my heart
I started making plans
To teach you what you'd need to know
To take the world by hand.

I want to spend each day with you,
Showing you how to live
To make this world a better place
Through all the love you'll give.

I may never be a shining star
Or change the world's grand scheme,
But I hope the love I show you
Will live on eternally.

I hope the strength you'll see in me
Will grow inside of you
And that honesty will guide you
And keep your heart so true.

You are my greatest legacy
My beautiful girl of mine.
Through you I'll live forever;
My light will always shine.

Shine through your eyes so big and brown
And through your smile so bright

And through each kiss and every hug
Through every prayer goodnight.

You are the reason I live a life
Fearlessly and bold
So that you'll always be proud of me.
My hand you'll want to hold.

Throughout your life you'll always know
Just what you mean to me.
You are my greatest love of all,
My darling legacy.

Jamie Johnson Turner
Aiken, SC
3rd Place

# DETERMINED

She cooks, she cleans.
She is a one-woman army with no one on her team.
She works hard to pay the bills.
This sister does not know how having a break feels.

After a hard day of laboring at her nine-to-five, she has to help
her children with their homework.
She smiles on the outside,
but inside this sister is hurt.

She regrets the bad decisions she made in her life.
She had dreams of having a two-parent home where she had a
strong husband, and she was a strong wife.
That was not reality, so she did what she had to do.
Her mother had been through the same as she, so this situation
was not new.

When her children were sick, she was the on-call doctor who was
up all night.
She had to provide for her children
even when money was tight.
She was all alone.
She had no one to call on when
she picked up the phone.
She held her head up high
even when she wanted to shed tears.

She believed in the most high; therefore, she was not worried,
and she did not have any fears.
She is a phenomenal woman unlike any other.
She is a superwoman better known to us as a single mother.

Jacqueline Renee Gonder
Augusta, GA
4th Place

# SENIOR WINNERS

# A POEM

Unlike troubles, poems come single spy,
not in battalions. A shadow meanders
the byways of the mind, contemplates
the hedgerows, picks wild word posies,
pokes in memory's ditches, crams its pockets
with noun nuts and verb berries,
makes its way to the uplands,
spreads a clean cloth,
tips out its hoard
and makes patterns with it.

At first it tries too hard,
later toys more patiently,
seems to lose interest, turns away,
seeking more success with other games
but can't help
glancing out of the corner of its eye,
testing possibilities.

Then, quite suddenly,
shadow no more,
and it is written, by itself,
on that clean cloth.

Joe Massingham
Chisholm, Australia
1ˢᵗ Place

# FOURTH OF JULY FAMILY REUNION

Setting out Aunt Olive's chicken, Les' melon basket, tea,
and some Italian in-law's tortellini, we stop all our mobility
to pay attention to the eight remaining elders, their dear
indomitability.

"The Thirteen," as we still call the siblings, had a lifetime
of difficulty. "The Great Depression? Whew! A time you don't
want to hear about, but since I'm

started now..." Friends that I have brought in
have laughed how, when they call for photo-taking, the eldest kin
are "kids."
We're grand and our kids are great. It means, under the skin,

we all began with Bess and Harry, a well-wed pair with manifold
capacity for taking care. The four youngest of their fold
are World War II vets, but don't call them old,

and don't expect star-spangled frou-farrah, group games or any
speech.
We have cousins catching up, showing off strawberry pie and
peach—

and how good that oldest child is to his sister.  We talk to each
aunt and uncle; despite three who worked in factories and no
longer hear,
one oxygen tank, six canes, a Chemo-damaged appetite, both
mild and severe
Alzheimer's, they meet here every year to do as they have always
done: to persevere.

Diane Kendig
Canton, OH
2nd Place

# ELDER'S LAMENT

Don't tell me I'm doing well for my age.
Don't pat me and call me 'dear.'
Don't say I should be glad I've lived so long,
That's not what I want to hear.

I want you to ask what I'm reading these days,
What I think about world affairs.
Don't assume I don't think anymore
Just because my knees can't manage the stairs.

I want my opinion to matter to you,
The way it used to be.
I may not look like the person you remember.
Inside I'm still the same me.

Don't look at the wall when you're talking to me,
As if I wasn't there.
Look straight into my eyes,
Make me feel that you care.

I want to be noticed again,
With a nod, a word or a smile.
Let me pretend I'm important,
For just a little while.

Ruth Merriman
Aiken, SC
3rd Place

# DANGER KEEP OFF SUBMERGED OBJECTS

No punctuation: no hesitant colon
comma coughing caveat
so
I ask the gulls how
the miller's daughter can spin
flaw into gold. Everything's hidden,
suggests the ring-billed beak,
standing his house
on sand.

But there's a man
skimming the shore with a straw detector,
looking for danger.
Think the queer motions
of a faith healer
floating his hands over a body,
or a monarch curing scrofula,
the royal touch—
Doesn't seems to be
finding much—

We all hide something,
but what did the king expect
when he took
the miller's chaff to bed.
Her face was her fortune
and then unhidden.

Meanwhile the water shimmies
over itself,
sinking what
lies beneath,
the gold crucifix
some lost swimmer lost
with his faith.

Well, says my therapist friend,
the danger comes
when you start talking.
Repression keeps us going.
We stand on the rocks
we cannot bear.

The miller's daughter,
it is said,
did not mention Rumplestiltskin
after she said his name,
developed carpal tunnel syndrome
in his stead.
No more spinning for the queen.
Disease too
riddles our skins.
Tuberculosis.
That kind of danger deep beneath.

Lois Marie Harrod
Hopewell, NJ
4th Place

# 2012 Judges

Gina Behr currently works as a Medical Assistant for Center for Primary Care. She was a judge for the adult category. Behr currently resides in Evans, GA.

Jessica Clark has been with Poetry Matters since its inception in 2000. She is currently studying Communications at Arizona State University. She volunteered as a judge for the middle school category.

Lucinda Clark is the co-founder and contest coordinator for Poetry Matters. This year, she judged the high school category. She is an award-winning publisher and founder of P.R.A. Publishing. While working to promote poetry, she has also been able to work with authors from all over the globe. Clark currently resides in Martinez, GA.

R. Xavier Clark began working as assistant editor for P.R.A. Publishing in 2006. He has worked with Poetry Matters since its inception. He judged the high school category and has worked on development of the annual awards program. He is currently studying business at the University of Georgia.

Ira Harrison, PhD was an activist during the 1960s and is currently an anthropologist and author. He has received his bachelor's degree at Morehouse College, his master's degree at Atlanta University, his PhD at Syracuse University, and his Master's of Public Health at John Hopkins University. Harrison's poems have appeared in publications such as The Phoenix and The Pegasus. He has also published six books of poetry. Harrison was a judge for the senior category and currently resides in Atlanta, GA.

Collin Kelley is the author of the new poetry collection, Render, out now from Sibling Rivalry Press. He is also the author of the mystery/suspense novel Remain In Light, a 2012 finalist for the Townsend Prize for Fiction, and Conquering Venus, both from Vanilla Heart Publishing. Kelley is the recipient of the 2007 Georgia Author of the Year/Taran Memorial Award and the 1994 Deep South Writers Award from the University of Louisiana. Kelley judged the senior category and currently resides in Atlanta, GA.

Takisha Perry is a published poet, talk show host and literary arts promoter. She has published several titles to date including When She Motions Hit the Page. She has toured all over the southern U.S. promoting her books and can be found on her talk show Kisha's Korner. Perry became a judge in 2010 for the adult category and currently resides in Augusta, GA.

Lisa Rosier has been a judge for the middle school category since 2007. She has been a Certified Medical Assistant with Center for Primary Care for 17 years. When she is not judging, she enjoys shopping, singing, and spending time with family and friends. She currently resides in Evans, GA.

Sharon Schroeder is a published poet, professor and literary arts advocate. She published her first title, Salt Water Blues, in 2010. She teaches English at Augusta Technical College and has served as editor of the Greater Augusta-Fort Gordon newsletter. She has been a judge and advocate of Poetry Matters since 2006; this year she judged for the high school category. Schroeder currently resides in Evans, GA.

NC Weil published her first novel, Karmafornia, in 2010. She has served as President of the Women's National Book Association: Washington D.C. chapter and is currently editor of the chapter newsletter, Signature. Her stories have appeared in Electric Grace and ArLiJo. This is her second year as a judge for Poetry Matters; she judged the senior category. Weil currently resides in Denver, CO.

Donna Weir-Soley was born and grew up in Jamaica. She currently teaches at Florida International University. She is a poet and critic and has been widely published in journals such as Caribbean Writer, Sage, The Carrier-Pidgin, Frontiers and in the anthology Moving Beyond Boundaries. She has also had a poetry book published entitled First Rain. This is Weir-Soley's first year judging for Poetry Matters; she judged the adult category. Weir-Soley currently resides in Miami, FL.

# About Poetry Matters

Mission Statement:
We believe the intent to act ethically, clarity of guidelines, and transparency of process form the foundation of an ethical contest. To that end, we agree to:

1.  Conduct our contest as ethically as possible.

2.  Provide clear and specific contest guidelines; defining conflict of interest for all parties involved.

3.  Make the mechanics of our selection process available to the public.

Contest History:
Poetry Matters began in 2000 as Dawning on the Riverwalk, a contest designed to showcase middle school poets. The contest gradually began encompassing more categories: first high school, then adults, and finally seniors. In 2008, after several years of trial and error and a proclamation made by county commissioners, the contest officially became Poetry Matters. The entity continued to progress, and, in 2011, we received more global entries than ever. Poetry Matters is still growing; we only hope that our poets and their fans will continue to support that growth.

# Anthology Series

The first Poetry Matters anthology showcases the 2009-2010 winners of the annual Poetry Matters contest. The contributors are residents of the Southeast (Georgia and South Carolina). They represent poets from middle school ages to senior citizens. The anthology is part of the Poetry Month celebration for P.R.A. Publishing with cash prizes provided by Center for Primary Care.

ISBN: 978.0982140727 trade paper

---

Power of Words is the second edition celebrating the program that showcases the winners of the annual Poetry Matters contest. These winners represent every aspect of life: middle school, high school, adults, and senior citizens. The poems show the power of poetry in moving, funny, and creative ways.

ISBN: 978.098214014200 trade paper

ISBN: 978.0982140789 e-book

Poetry Diversified showcases the compiled experiences of the 2012 Poetry Matters Contest winners. The anthology is filled with language that bears the souls of twenty-three poets with twenty-three different stories to tell. The title says it all; these writers represent diversities in age, gender, religion and every type of social category, which their various experiences represent. All poets take their readers through different emotional peaks and valleys, from sorrow and guilt to discovery, hope, and joy. Poetry Diversified will suit the tastes of anyone who is stirred by emerging poetic voices.

ISBN: 978-0984014231 trade paper

www.ingramcontent.com/pod-product-compliance
Lightning Source LLC
Chambersburg PA
CBHW032052040426
42449CB00007B/1083